LABYRINTH

D1739146

Labyrinth

by

Sybil Pittman Estess

Pecan Grove Press San Antonio, Texas

Cover art by Robert Ferre, reprinted with permission

Author photograph by Jay Brashears, reprinted with permission.

ISBN: 978-1-931247- 41-2

Pecan Grove Press
Box AL
1 Camino Santa Maria
San Antonio, TX 78228

Acknowledgments

(Grateful acknowledgment to the journals in which the following poems were published, some in slightly different form.)

Borderlands: "What the Citizens of Texas Need"

Langdon Review of the Arts: "Black Eye," "Clear, Fall Day," "Florida, Grayton Beach," "From South Mississippi," "Galveston," "My Mother's Doors," "Rhymes on Albuquerque"

Main Street Rag: "Montana Moon"

Mutabilis: "My Love Affair With Diane Sawyer"

Open Windows (Texas A&M University English Department Internet Journal): "Rhymes on Albuquerque"

RATTLE: "The Crisis Angel"

Shade 2006: "Abstraction" (published as "Destruction of Names")

WOMEN'S JOURNAL (Brigid's Place Women's Center, Christ Church Episcopal Cathedral, Houston): "Labyrinth, Fourteen Ways"

For my mother, deeply missed

Marion Sybil Stringer Pittman Cochran
(1921-2003)

CONTENTS

I. Morning Star

II. How Heathcliff Misses Passion

III. Labyrinth

"We take what's given and work
with that. The rest is grace."

W. S. Di Piero—"Some Voice"

I

MORNING STAR

THE CRISIS ANGEL

OK, she said, I will get you through this.
Dressed in rosy pink, she kept pulling me
through multiplied crises, one after
the next. Would mother live? Wouldn't
she? Was I going to get there in time?
Which plane? What would I find?
(I'd never been in an ICU.)
                                    Look,
the angel said, "It's going to get worse
but you'll make it." I liked her a lot,
her dainty hair, yellow as corn-silk.
Her dress, immaculate, the color
of first wild spring rose. Her will, tough.
She wouldn't take a pill. No Miltown.
Didn't even drink white wine. I'd never
cared for pink before. Thought it meant
not being able to face what's real. See,
she said, what it means to be fully female?
You'll be able to bend on the spot. You
can be a displaced person at the drop
of a hat—yet not forget who you are.

Remember the Jews in Babylon? Prisoners
who wouldn't confess? Read about Lot's
wife, frozen because she looked back.
Recall Odysseus stuck on the island, he too
wanting to go home. Think of Penelope.
Job. (He refused to curse God even for
his wife.) Picture Christ. Did you know
I was there that day fanning his fever? Back
then, my garb was white and sexless. Now,
I am Eve, Esther, Marys—Mother, Magdalene.

She stayed with me, since I couldn't shed her.
We went to K-Mart, close to the hospital
and cheap. I bought some temporary clothes
to wear as captive. My exile. Everything
pink: pajamas, slacks, sweater for cool,
crystalline April there. Underwear. I have
learned that pink is powerful. And I am
growing my own puffy pink wings, sweet
as cotton candy. I am becoming my dear
crisis angel. I live in the instant. My husband,
son, city, house, job, clothes, garden, poems—
my life—are far away back home. But now,

I sit at the head of the bed of sick and dying.
I bind the red wounds of my relatives, friends.
I pray five times a day to nourish strength.
I praise. I sculpt and mold whatever comes.

Outside the Door at ICU

We all line up at 10:00 a.m. in silence,
waiting as if going before the throne of God,
who presides over the highest court on earth.

We do not know what we will find behind
these doors except soap and hot water to scrub
our hands. Beyond double doors, tubes,

bottles and electric monitors are not sleeping.
(This is the post-modern age of life in crisis saved
or prolonged.) We eye each other. No one smiles

or speaks but me. ("And yours?" I say. "Seventy
days." "Progress?" "She still doesn't know me."
"You have who?" "My wife in a car-wreck."

"Children?" "Three kids at home." "Are you working?"
"Yes. I leave and come here at six; ten; two; six; ten.")
We clock the hours when they will not lock us out.

The young black girl with lupus dies. Her family
of fourteen in the waiting room leaves.
The young man's wife still does not know him.

The old man's wife, who's been here eight months
with heart failure, does. He feeds her. On Tuesday
Mother responds, begins to breathe without machines.

We stop searching for her living will at home.
On Thursday she's wheeled out to her
penthouse room. Yesterday, as I passed ICU,

5

a young woman emerged. She screamed all the way
to a car, leaning on the shoulder of her young, male
friend. "Would you like to sit her down here

to calm her?" I say. "I'm alright! I'm alright!" The halls
echo as she walks and wails and sobs. He holds her.
They leave out the same automatic door that connects

us to the elevated parking garage, where
all the nine-month pregnant women and I
walk or waddle in.

LINKS

A man weeps when his ninety-six-year-old aunt
begins to die. She can't come to his son's

wedding. He is crying while he is trying
to emcee his son's rehearsal dinner

ceremony at the Tex-Mex cafe in Houston
the night before the big wedding day.

That great aunt was coming here
until this week. Doctors say she has cancer.

One guest says, "Why does he cry when she is
so old? Shouldn't he have expected it?

Doesn't he have other relatives here?"
Yes, so many! Other relatives, friends,

people to fill spaces in his large heart.
Yet see him as all of us who are "linked."

I lost my mother from her home last week.
"But you never lived there. It's not where you

were raised. Your mother has had a good life.
She's lived well, long. Be glad for memory.

Get on with it. Look at good sides. Be brave,"
people repeat. I reply to those clichés:

"Links are not rational. Links know no age.
Memories cannot replace them—nor time.

Not counting blessings. Nor good days, good friends.
Cousins. Coupons. Bank statements. Balances.

Tears are first prayers
we pray when we have no more."

I Have No Story / I Have No Tale

In The Great Depression in Mississippi,
her grandparents who owned
a cotton gin went broke that year,
1927, the Mexican boll weevil came.
Her own father, son-in-law with five
kids already, an itinerant preacher,

followed suit in *Grapes of Wrath* style.
They all tied mattresses on Model-T
tops and were caravans to California
looking for work. On the way, they
camped out, ate from cans, slept two
weeks under stars in Texas, New Mexico,

Arizona. She was six when she first
picked in cotton and orange fields.
They first lived in big canvas tents
she chose not ever in her life to recall.
She didn't remember the cots, either,
the ones her two living sisters did,

on which they first slept. She did see
she was the one who kept the three
younger kids—especially when
that last baby came. Their mom worked
in a peach cannery. "It wasn't like that,"
she contradicted them. "That would have

made us like migrant workers. We weren't."
"Yes, yes we were . . . for a while. . . ."
"No," she said, "No. I was never that.
That's not my memory. Mine is something
else." "What?" they asked. "What? How is it
different?" "I don't know," she answered.

9

"I don't remember that far back . . . but I claim
none of that." So mother did not own
her own story. She wouldn't put her name
on her pain. Some other, perhaps—but
she didn't say, didn't know which.
Her history, then, was not that of her sisters,

which is my inheritance that I heard from them.
As for her, she lived in the moment,
the present being the only place she believed
people should stay. "Why look back?" she argued.
"Even if it ever happened, it might
or might not be true. Who knows what took place,

what's real? I don't. They don't. You don't.
Don't you agree?"

Houston, Back Alone
(After Columbia's fall)

From Denton to see my paralyzed, mute
mother. On Saturday, there, like Icarus,

Columbia's seven soared overhead, then
floated down like feathers. I overheard

the news from the nursing home's
priest. Last year, I remembered that

my husband's brother, a NASA director,
signed five of this crew's permits

to go. That morning at 8:00 a.m.,
I had talked to my cousin in Plano. She had seen

the silver bird, high, knew nothing.
Afterward, I walked the nursing home's lake

path around brown water, looked for brown
geese, always there. They were gone. . . . But before

the knowledge of this new sorrow,
I breathed endless blue (clear as September 11

in Manhattan) Texas air. Saw a man
on a motorized, happy-colored parasail

wave down to me, smiling. Saw a blue heron
I must have startled from its nest. It rose,

became as wide as a human body is long. Then
ascended up, up into the neutral, unknowing sky.

Today, speeding south on I-45
toward home, in my car, I see on the right

side of the road two yellow roped-off pieces
of the ship. Now there are 2,800 miles of glowing

charred debris.

My Mother's Doors

After Mother's first strokes, she'd watch
for me at the front door or in the wooden
porch glider of the Denton home
for assisted living.

Then that major stroke.
Those heavy doors we pushed to get
to her: paralyzed, waiting.

We wheeled her past doors
to bright caged birds so many
nursing homes buy.

She managed
to move her eyes, only. Later,
lungs collapsing,
no food tubes
for two weeks, motionless
but groaning so painfully that all
nurses on the bright hall wept,
Mother passed through her
last door at nearly midnight.

I am tempted
to want my mother back
waiting at doors
of all her Mississippi homes,
welcoming me
even if she cannot ever
again be whole.

The Altar Is Stripped

(for George Dougherty, remembered well)

Maundy Thursday—day before Jesus died.
The church eats its last Eucharist

until Easter. Communicants kneel in the dark.
In the sanctuary, priests enter. They start

to dismantle the altar. First the Bible,
next, candelabrum, leaving gloom.

Last, the crosses, signaling our loss
from north/south/east/west. Everything,

even cushions, where we kneel for the body
and blood are taken too. Final gestures:

celebrants lift their arms, taking the lingering
linen off. (Like shrouds used to wrap you

and Christ for your rest.) What they say is
on Sunday things will look different. Then

they will rip that black gauze off the only cross
left. We'll sing alleluias again, amid white

lilies. Churches say losing is how we are
redeemed. So I am trying to imagine what

cleansing I needed that your death gave me.
What sins were taken from me by seeing

your chilled pale body stopped still. How you
there endlessly in that grave lifted my every flaw

away. How having you, having to give you up,
healed. You taught us what we know: "Let go.

Let go. Let it all . . . let me . . . slowly go."

SINCE ONE OF THEM WAS DYING
(Raymond Carver and Tess Gallagher)

Tess said that first, like two serpents, they
shed the old skin, dry and tattered with use.

Then they reduced fat pad, even those
solitary sinews, fibrous muscles, strength

that once gave false hope of control.
Next they sloughed off separate arteries,

isolated veins. What flowed to one heart
came to the tough pump of the partner.

They deigned to be friends, besides lovers.
True mates. The diagnosis sealed their fate.

All would end—not late but soon. Yet
their whole fall was a gift. It was as if they

had lifted to a light place with no end.
Chemotherapy could not heal like this did.

They faced each day feeling that all others
(brothers, races) could live likewise:

arrive at the place of "No Single Self."
Their giving was gain. (I ask: *Was it sane,*

or just more magically real than Marquez
or Allende to sob from their throbbing cores,

so connected. Making beauty, guessing truth?)
She said they thought of love, power

there's no more.

STUCK BIRDS DREAM

She lives in a cold, high place in the Rockies,
the sublime she'd tried to reach in many dreams.
She's built a house and moved there to the peak.
She can see all the bright sights she'd longed for.
Now she sits all day, looking. Noon she leaves
her site to buy food. Just as soon as
she escapes, a meteorite hits it, missing
her on the walk. Calamity can come
any moment, she thinks, crush flat all
she came here for. It can harrow her house
on the tip-top of a peak. Then she gazes up,
sees pink clouds, cheery, bright, girlish,
Disney-like. Yet huge black crows peck
the pink puffs to pieces, slowly. So crows grow
to resemble an Ernst or a Magritte.

All the while, her stepfather fades
and the malignant tumor takes
his last lung. He stays painfully chained
to his lost life much too long.

"Thanatos," the crows say when she asks them
their name. They speak detached, and devour
the pink moisture they seem glued to. "Shoo!"
she says. "Shoo! Won't you leave here? Won't you
let this pink float in peace?" But that blue
canvas is still stuck, sucked by rooks, black
and cannibal.

Fire and sooty earth meet to eat
water. Gone, gone is all holy air.

GALVESTON

It's a fogged-in night in late November,
her birthday. One of Jane's friends just died.

She sits on a pied third floor balcony
over a loud, southern sea. The fiery ocean,

this fierce fog could be in California
or Devon, if it were not just Texas, fifty miles

from Jane's home. Multi-colored boardwalk lights
shine through like a long Christmas tree,

foretelling the holidays. This motel is built
on tall steel stilts drilled down through sand.

Jane came here to rest from land, to count
the rest of her life and to plan.

To listen, hear what certain seas say.
They say fog. They say white-topped water

mountains made by wind, by whatever else
makes patterned tide. They say rhythm.

Lightning flashes far beyond her—out near
specters of jutting oil rigs. At dawn, white gulls

circle, squawk, feed by her room's open door
where Jane Clare sits in clear air in a rose-flannel

robe sipping coffee. By the time the sun sears
at seven, the stirring sea has sent her secrets

it keeps. It tells her all the knowledge
on earth, in its loud, wordless way.

Morning Star

It was not the sea that brought them down off
Newport or Long Island. Don't blame the sea.
It was the land with its mistakes that made us
grieve Flight 990 and Pan Am's downed plane.

And when the hurricanes howled, we knew it was
not the sea: neutral, gravitized, creature-containing.
For some restless selves the sea soothes with its laps
and rhythm, its engulfing otherness. Its daily change.

So, Mother, I came to the sea to mourn
for the loss of you and the home you gave
me for fifty-six years—in Mississippi.
Then your mind would not let your body stay.

The lonely house, lovely, sits empty now.
Each of your paintings you put on your walls.
Each china cup and collection of tiny jewels
still arranged on dusty shelves. Light still pours

in the sun room where you sat so much, seeing
bluebirds at bird feeders, wrens splashing
in birdbaths you kept full even when you could
not keep yourself. The TVs, radios are not turned

on. Your bed does not have a body to hold.
Your refrigerator has no pies. Your plants
die, dry. Your Mercury has its battery
going down. I pay neighbors to cut grass

and rake fall leaves. "What everyone must do
with grief," some say blithely, "is ritualize it."
So I came here for thirty days bringing
one Jerusalem candle to this shore. But

at night I see out the glass doors more lights
than I knew about or had expected:
oil rigs, shrimp boats, huge ships lining up
to go into port. One regular show rises

nightly, quite early: Venus from the East
moving slowly over southern horizon until
dawn. Sometimes with our moon at her side.
Often alone, I am alone now. "Middle-aged

orphans," some call us who are now asked
to allow the last parent to go. The home where
we placed our mother is named "Morning Star."
Mother, my Venus, you are with me through

black nights. Then in daylight,
with the aching memory,
I wait for that bright planet to reappear.
Sign of impossible loss, morning star.

II

HOW HEATHCLIFF MISSES PASSION

How Heathcliff Misses Passion in Pensacola

He cannot count the ways as these countless
waves crash. He misses trying to speak

the nature of poetry—though that has now
passed. He misses Cath's long hair, her laugh.

He sees a blonde woman tromping the sand,
and for moments he imagines her:

Catherine. She too would be graying; her waist
would have grown. Today's sun has risen. The air

is like spring. How many nights in this blue-
moon month has he dreamed of her again

in some guise—the dear one, his daemonic.
Perhaps he has now become her.

Yet he misses her, if just as myth. Her
real husband is in the other room. Was Edgar,

though, her other half? Or was it Heathcliff?
Maybe they were Plato's dream. Never skin

between them, only soul. It seems many kinds
of love are love. He called her, always, love.

And love and love and loves. He misses telling
Catherine about a book on this blue-green beach,

each day extreme and changing. And of course
the pink dawns he tries not to miss.

Some days fog, all day, sun foiled. Ships anchored
white and lighted at night, as in Coleridge's

"Rhyme" and its albatross. This wet
mystery, like love, is without time.

This morning the brown-suited kayaker
rises and falls on gray swells. Yesterday,

twenty-five shark-like surfers. Last week, bright
and light-blue transparent beached jellyfish

of all eerie sizes. Gray or white gulls
who cheer and devour them. Circuitous

cycle. The storm coming from Mexico
casts mad water fifteen feet from these

small green block houses built in the '50s.
Schools of dark dolphins surface

to breathe, rise and dive. Nearly daily,
flying so low, pelicans search for fish

while tiny, nervous sandpipers
peck beside endless clear tide.

He misses Catherine's talking. Her talk, talk.
Her sassiness, her asking him about his

children, his spouse, the dense rest of his
dark double life.
                    So even if she

despised him, his past, willful dear one,
he still misses her puns.

Her absence is present and palpable.
A cruel gift. (So many gifts between them.)

This is the first poem by Heathcliff here
in Pensacola—meaning "five colors" of salt

water, like his excessive, passionate tears.

Years Later

"But we don't live our lives so much
as come to them," the story says. "As
people and things collect mysteriously

around us." How Heath collected around
Cath, or she around him, like the nuance
of fog that she loved. He loved her voice

and her care for his words. Heathcliff
loved what Catherine saw as her soul.
Now they would both be so old. Does she

imagine him, ever? Does she remind herself
how she once told him she could not live
without him? Before her death . . . that now seems

brief, and immaculate. Is it true: we do
not live our lives so much as come to them—
like an accident that is not one? (Why

did her father save him?) Like the lives
of the stars, moon, and sun—that time,
those moors, two too passionate pasts.

Perhaps All His Life

had led up to this. Perhaps all his life
has prepared Heathcliff for how to face her

on the heath. Who is he? And what must
he face? He who has loved too much since

Liverpool, has not demanded enough.
Catherine, whom he has tried to peck open—

as this bird, this red-headed woodpecker,
tries to peck open the tree.

When his father would not respond,
he should have learned how to let go.

When his mother did not praise him, he should
have relinquished his obsession with accolades.

Is Heath forgoing it only now? He pats
his own back, lives without adoration.

The kinds of love and quantity he has craved.
See: he wills not to dream of Catherine. He wants

to rest, nights and days.

ABSTRACTION

Catherine once loved dancing.
She can remember lush
waltzes and eros. She would follow Heath

to his car, not bother to name what they felt.
Found her lover's hand, raised it to her breast.
Only now, no passion to build on, only her

lonely poems. Has Cath become an abstraction?
Does naming kill the soul, slowly, as it labels?
Can Catherine descend again to flowering earth,

glowing and showing by sun, or moon?

House of Spirits
(after Isabel Allende)

Women are the ones who know spirits. Men,
their lovers, never see what is unseen.

Clara talks to ghosts, gives birth, with her mother's
severed head seeing her from the top of the chest.

The girl she bears has green hair like Clara's
dead sister who was poisoned

by her father's political rivals. Enemies meant
the rat poison for him. Seeing her sister's autopsy

through the window (sister laid out on kitchen
table), Clara goes mute at age nine.

At nineteen, she married her sister's lover she never
liked (although he adores her, even as he knocked

her teeth out in rage). Clara wears her false teeth
on a string around her neck the rest of her life. She never

speaks to him again. It is a world of magic, as
in all of our lives: everything senseless, yet real.

Two Haiku on Love

1: *The Rose*

Crimson meets my eye,
deceives: what blood beneath your
luscious, fence-like leaves?

2: *The Image Slashed*

The mirror shattered
never again reflects. Now
who are you to me?

Likenesses

In the image Heathcliff holds,
she is a mirror. In his undying

vision, he kisses her toes, calves,
breasts in some hidden way.

He rubs her aching elbows.
He knows this: she would have grown

older, distant and gray. (Perhaps
someday she will be with him, but how?)

Even now, she speaks another
language: death. No, all things about

the two of them were always so remote.
They both knew. But Catherine's other

realm he can't see. Her stasis
mends desire. Before, craving nothing

at all, except his black grin. And what
sin he seemed to see or say. All that

quick newness they were and gave so
freely to their own likenesses. Yesterday.

Withering Script

Casually, Heathcliff has Catherine cornered
by candle-light, margaritas and whiskey. No
other souls in the barroom. She sits with her back

to West Gray Street. Windows show sunset.
This is October autumn. In fall, two
years past, all Act II began. They speak

of the three acts of them: beginning, middle
and end. "In the middle, you were in love
with me," Cath says. "Act I and Act II," Heath

answers, "are both done." No, she hadn't intended
to weep, to keep folding and unfolding her
paper napkin until she had torn it to bits.

"No," she says, "we are still in Act II."
True, there has been no curtain. Middles move
upward, then crescendo. Act IIIs all start

to slide straight down to denouement.
"And you?" Heath asks. "Your heart?"
"It could be," Cath answers, "I have loved you.

It could be I still do even now. Yet— " They are
losing youth. Their real lives have a hundred
twists: Edgar's moors, houses, their past

status quos, loves, locations. Two questions:
"If Act I is over, as agreed, will Act III simply
come as it can?" (Or will Act II never end?)

RHYMES ON ALBUQUERQUE

What a clear, cool night in Albuquerque.
Old Town's not at all cold for February.

Since sixteen, working in Santa Fe, Cath has
loved this desert. She thinks it's a treasure-trove

of turquoise, adobe, chile, with dry
air and moonlight. Tonight, winter sky

does not disappoint. But she's far from home
in Houston, and her husband. She has roamed

from her demented mother, moved to Texas
now. Deep lack makes her hate this feckless

midnight. Silence in the high plains is so lonely.
The snow on the Sandìa range (for only

her) such a waste—and her eros. Soon
she walks back to La Quinta, forlorn.

Tomorrow to the shops—the Navajo
and Zuni bright blue stones. The patio

at the Church Street Cafe where coffee is
piñon, delicious. Hot tamales sheer bliss.

But tonight, Catherine sees Venus, her star.
She wants Heathcliff to say, "Yes, you are."

S-Eros

When you are young, wanting a mate,
it's *s-eros* taking you to her eyes
with long black lashes, or to his

talks about microbiology or Heidegger.
We yearn for the Other. But are we
chewed, swallowed, lost? What cost

drew you to the moon, you a mere
satellite? Now you've forgotten
some of the foods you liked, your

family, your original name. Could
there be a new marriage for two?
A new kind of love? Call it

s-eros. S-eros would sink you
deeper into your own depths
than you've dived before. *S-eros*

would be *philios* too—brotherly,
sisterly love. The other would want
what you desire for you. The wedding

ceremony might say: "Do you promise
that?" You do not need to think of what
the children will say your devotion was.

For they will recall you as you do: two
pitchers. They'll know you poured each
other water often. But you kept saying,

S-eros.

My Love Affair with Diane Sawyer

Who's to say it's only a one-way street?
Maybe she intuits the fact that I love her.

Why do I? I am not lesbian, though
no doubt I project quite a lot. (They say,

"She's my good shadow.")
See: she's up every morning and looking

more than great by the time my feet hit floors.
She is gorgeous. (I crave her haircut!)

My husband, of course, says she's sexy—
as we sit sipping caffeine, surveying

how the Clintons have goofed, or George W.,
Arabs, Israelis. Another thing about Diane:

she is completely equal to her man—
her co-anchor. They sit side by side. No

patronizing—no Jane Pauley baby-doll. No
Walters who has grown too old and also

has a crooked mouth. Ms. Sawyer is so
totally cool. Can't you tell—she knows

everything on every issue,
goes into the hardest, hot-spot places

all over the globe. Arafat's office,
when she is drenching wet and rain has poured.

(She never even gets sick—no sniffles!)
She doesn't get panicked, as I do, flying.

She stopped an Israeli army convoy
by the side of the Jerusalem road

in her British khakis—her hair blowing
but never a ratty mess. She forges

into prisons. She comforts. She confronts.
She is one wonder woman! I love looking

at her clothes—and thank God for color
T.V. This morning she had on an aqua shell

blouse and black tights, black rubber-sole flats.
I often gaze (as my spouse does) at her long,

lovely legs, today covered. I found out
the reason. This woman wizard can dance—

on ice, outside ABC studio
in NYC on an ice rink. (Diane did

not seem too cold, since she is oh so
adaptable.) She's not the slightest bit

racist. She was dancing with an Afro-American
dance group. Not missing a beat. Knew each

turn to take, black topper-coat matching her
pants. The whole U.S. sees her—maybe even

the world. I want my hairdresser to make
my locks look like Diane's. I am thinking

of bleaching my hair blonde like hers. (Oh yes:
she's thin.) Diane is not even divorced,

and as far as I can see she has no issues
with men. Jane Pauley left her husband. Long

before that, poor Jessica Savitch drowned. Other
female anchors seem to suck up, or come on

much too strong, talk wrong, don't have
that raspy voice Diane has, driving my husband

wild. He sees her, I know, for childish sex. To me
Sawyer has everything a female should have

in the 21st century: fame, money, looks, brains,
power, guts, animus, all. I don't know

her score on wholeness or integration.
But as for TV, she's A-1 for me.

JESUS AT THE PAGODA

Marching toward me are sixty National
Guardsmen with multi-pitched catcalls
assailing. Golfers on greens knock balls.

(The Sunday afternoon poetry reading
is finished. I intend a long, lonely walk
in a Houston park. But our city is packed.)

So a teen-age biker almost bumps me.
Six girl joggers go by, puffing like fillies.
I hear cars honk, leaving the zoo:

Fords, Chevrolets, Mercedes stack at the stuck
red light. Beside the path one tattooed Asian
practices Tai Chi. A black female athlete

teaches her partner warm-ups, circling her thin
arms and neck. Then "*Vamonos! Vamonos!*" dins
a Latino mother to two toddlers digging in dirt.

Rose gardens burst upon view with bright yellow
tea roses, orange Floribunda, red Chrysler
Imperial, Crimson Glory, Pascali. Next

to these are purple thrift, pink Gerber daisies,
carnations, verbenas, zinnias. I say I will
plant all this in my own garden—but I must

have said this before. I catch sight of an Asian
wedding on a lawn: white tiered cake under a gold
pagoda on green St. Augustine grass. The crowd

and couple are amber-skinned, round-faced
with thin black eyes. Is this dark bride
in flowing white gown and veil

Shinto or Buddhist? I wonder. What music?
Then I hear it: their soft, Taiwanese Baptist
voices sing, "Softly and Tenderly Jesus

Is Calling," and "I'll Fly Away" in English.
"When the trumpet of the Lord shall sound
and time shall be no more. . . ."

It is only March. I imagine November, December
to come with some cold, brown, manageable
order I want desperately in Texas this spring.

But today
I keep walking into color and chaos.
Tai Chi juxtaposed with Jesus at the gold

 pagoda. Converted Chinese amid Latino.
"*Vamonos! Vamonos!*" (Let's go!) Into my
 musings of Giacometti's thin, bones-

only people who keep moving. Like them,
I go on by the one routine I know:
left foot, right foot. Left, right, left.

What the Citizens of Texas Need

I'm not sure what the citizens
need is passion.
I've been down to Palacios, have you?

I've spent a night in the Luther Hotel.
It is dead, finished as the fishing town,
ballroom, railway. Has one cafe

to eat fried cod in, or liver. I went on
Valentine's one year, so I had lots
of passion for poor Palacios. I began

to think I could live there, loving
water, breathing salt, sea air, skating
on the walkways by the bay. I could

eat in the cafe, wouldn't cook. I could
live in the Luther Hotel like a hobo,
two 1950s rooms I'd rent

for summer to write poems in all day.
I've also been to Rockport. I tried
to rent a boat there for my son. I found one

at a marina, gently Gentiled them down.
I have traveled to Corpus, too, seen those
beaches by palm trees on boardwalks

swaying like seductive dancers. I went
to Bryan, found some caring persons there
as well. (They knew a gal who gagged on passion,

nearly died.) Most of all, I have a friend
who grew up in Well Springs. She needed
nothing if not tenderness from her own

father, who raped her for ten years. He wasn't
short of heat. Perhaps it isn't passion we need
here in devastated Texas, or anywhere on earth.

What we starve for is com-passion, "suffering with,"
to guide us through solstices, darkness,
through our fifties, beyond. Yearning

for something we wish to keep
that's endless, worthy,
maybe true.

SONNET ON CONJUNCTIO
(for Ted)

What enticed us in, back then? We fell through
each other. At eighteen, I spilled my books,
and you bent down outside our choir room to
pick them up. "I will marry those good looks,"

I said to myself. You were a projection
of my female need: male, tall, all mysterious
in your silence. He needs me, I thought. Fun
was out of our question. We were so serious

then about metaphysical crises such as God
or Tillich's ground of being. Seeing, such students,
we burned to know—all things but us. We'd prod
each other in constant debate, what we meant:

new agnostics, late on long rides home. Did you have fears
I loved you? Marriage, books, faithfulness, forty years.

Don't Leave Him

Bring the fat, grit, dirt, grime,
pain of your heart. Your two
new locations—death and life.
Your old scars. Bring your

female soul with the dents
he has nailed. But if you
have to go, when you pack
the big bags you carry back

and forth forever, save one
small space. Fold Heathcliff
inside a clean Kleenex in a
pocket. He won't cost or talk

much. He will slip right by
security, and customs, Catherine.
(Poor guy: so silent in the cold casket.
He won't freeze, since he's hot

for you.) Please, if you can't
bring yourself and all your stuff
to relent and return to him here,
Cath, keep him in your care.

Moorings

When all new roads seem old,
too bumpy. When small stones
have taken up lodging
in your shoes, hurt your heels.
When kids are becoming
what they can be—you see
how little you can do,
really, for them now. You
know you still have left your last
moorings. What memory
will fade more? What winter
may come before autumn?
What places are yet
some deep pit? What
communion will still fill you?

III

LABYRINTH

CLEAR FALL DAY
(During memorials for 9/11/01)

Afterward she thinks of the poet Williams
who wrote, "So much depends. . . ."
On a September day. On clear air.

All instruments, check-points, seemed safe.
Everything, even the air, was fair. Yet it
was seen only one way. No white birds,

like spirit, appeared as they did to a seer
transforming his mere vision to sight.
(New summer farm-red.) No accidental

rain made one transparent raindrop that day.
That fall no one stopped by a road
to write. *This poem is against certainty.*

For the sadness of singleness, no rites.

BLACK EYE

When each possession had been swept
away by wind or water, and the chaos labeled
3, 4, or 5, death came. Or displacement.
What was left to salvage? No house, clothes,
photo to hold or help heal. Some survivors
waved white or red "Save Us" flags for several days.
Sometimes someone came to those rags or signs
by small boats. But refugees, rebuffed, had been struck
by the eye.
                Each of us now has been a host to some
lost child recalling when waters climbed higher.
Lush green gardens gone, and trees are salt-
watered at best. (The whole of horror is
not just tossed bombs.) So where can they flee
next from Pass Christian, Bay St. Louis, Waveland,
Gulfport, Biloxi, Ocean Springs, or New Orleans?
The lucky ones, left with breath.

FROM SOUTH MISSISSIPPI
(January, 2006)

Skies are gray today, tepid
January. Down the short hill
where I walk every winter here
the greenest rye grass usually grows.
Deer who are feasting see me if I appear
late evenings or early at sunrise. So
today I descend, expect the same pasture
and fish pond.

But the whole hamlet, it seems, has been recast.
This field is now full of dead, uprooted oaks
someone burned here as trash. Stumps smoke.
This year I find only ash and waste. Beyond, brown
buck may hide and stare from deep
in pines that the August storm left,
but I cannot see them. On my trek
past dry and rotting debris
of vines and brush piled high from Katrina,
one crimson cardinal against all the rest—then

that shock of pure black.

Montana Moon

The skin of the mountain sits on the moon.
Parched hills are arched elephants' backs, soon

one can imagine. Moonlight is a slivered lump
of sliced sugar, touching the brown hill's hump.

It sticks to a vast spill of blue ink—this
black night. Californians discover and kiss

air here that's unlike La Jolla's. They buy it.
Ranchers in irrigated valleys will split

profits from more retirees from Riverside.
Rattlers with thick venom adjust weathered hide

to real estate risings. They like to slither along.
Great grizzlies and big buck have no luck. For a song,

the damned BLM sells thick wilderness daily.
Missoula writers peck sleepless pages and palely

worry. The FBI, like squirrels, scurried
to armed mad militia. Meanwhile, unhurried,

the skin of the marvelous mountain, sinless,
sits on the great grinning Moon's forgiveness—

a bright, clear, colossal acceptance of all
this grandeur, before our timeless fall.

Colors and Wildlife: Grand Lake

Our two-year-old black bull moose with rack
lets my six-foot son sneak right up to snap him

by our lake. Deer from the Rockies devour
neighbors' white daisies, dusty from drought.

She shoos them away. Porcupines pooped last night
on our deck. Chipmunks on this roof run us nuts!

Quiet! We are trying to write! Amid park peaks—
Cumulus, Nimbus, Never Summer—last night coyotes

woke us in full moonlight, howling in the quarry.
Elk eat in herds here in green pastures nearly each night.

Peach-colored salmon, with lime at our table, were caught
in the Colorado River on my boy's new fly-rod hook.

Dark bear are hiding. But mist-covered horses trot,
carrying kids from back East to cook-outs at daybreak

across the dawn-broken field, frosty in sun-baked
wildflowers. What a lark! Columbine, too, rise blue

and lavender. One green hummingbird sips at my
red feeder, red-throated. Then twitters, flitters, and flies

into blue. In town, brown clown squirrels want free
hand-outs. They beg and beg. Then it snowed the last

night in July. Just after mid-summer, mountains white.

LEGACIES

How and what shall we leave
our kids? Some told histories?
House, stock, cash, thought.

Schools, memories and trips.
Holidays. Traditions. God?
Ancestors. Good childhoods.

Books. Terror? Good looks?
How to bequeath what? How shall
we leave them this earth? Stone

Mountain. Pearl River. Bird.
Marten. Lamprey. Lanceolate
leaf. Heat. Glacier. Morgan horse.

Birch trees, Blackfoot. Redwood.
Naming. (History: Native
Americans. Slaves. War. Camps.)

Icecaps. India. Gaza.
South Seas, Switzerland,
Sweden, Mexico. Wooster,

Massachusetts. Elves in Africa.
Imagination. Wisdom. Something
real?

Rebellion: Teenage

I am so angry at the cop
who doesn't give me a ticket.
I don't stop when I fender-

dent in the parking lot at last
Friday night's football game.
I am full of hate at my mother

who even though she works
and is usually busy and tired
keeps washing my clothes,

and at my dad who praises me
always and especially
after my failures. Also at my

girlfriend who talks all the time
and helps me with my homework
and whose mother is dying any

day now of pancreatic cancer.
Who needs her? I am daily
disgusted by the principal who

refuses to kick my ass all
the way out of my lousy,
unnecessary, uptight school.

Remembering Colors of the First Hit

She is female, five, and very lively.
Kate feels ecstatic most of the time.
Lots of green energy for things
like jumping, a change from making wet
gray mud pies in the unpainted wood sandbox

in her overalls, thick pink corduroy,
she remembers, blue cotton bonnet, white
lace around the rim of the brim's edges.
(There's a black and white snapshot of her
in that suit she still has in the picture book.)

Now it's late in the summer evening, after
work. (He might have been tired.) There are no
power mowers then—only hand-push—and
her dad is pushing hard. Kate is so happy she is
hopping: Daddy is home! She makes a game

of leaping right in front of his yellow
mower, seeing if she can race fast enough
to skip away before she lands in his line
of mowing. Kate hops high once right over
the rusty machine. She jumps one too many

times for her daddy's taste—or patience.
"If you don't quit, I'm going to take you
in the house to whip you," he scolded.
His words struck her Eden, like lightning,
began to tempt her to her first red rage—

perhaps like Daddy's own. Her daddy hit her?
But she had no time to think again—it all occurred
so quickly, like a flash. So soon that her sister
and mother stay outside. After she bounds

again, the final time, he hits her with his hand
in the kitchen, dragging her up their back-door
steps, inside. After that no words. No apology.
All things had ended—
her clear world, her carefree play. Her mother

said he did it before but for her it was new
memory. Sin. Soon she takes on another color:
black revenge. She has never, even now, got back
at him enough—made him see just what he did
to his daughter that summer night. It was the start

of something scarlet. But as in all her darkness,
soon she is somewhere in the middle, with no voice.
No one to plead her case—not even her mother.
With no one to say, "Let her keep her energy.
Let her jump clear across the moon if she can.

Let her smell that sweet summer grass. Let her
feel tan sand in her shoes. Let her keep pure
pleasure, please, just a little while longer."

OLDER DAUGHTER

He started to drink like a man nursing
knife blades. Whiskey smothered his fear.

He listened as if a dying bird croaked
his diagnosis. Not fatal. He made it

so. Then when his older daughter heard
his car horn honk after midnight under

their carport again, after midnight,
she gave in, called some upright neighbors.

In silence they lifted him into his house.
It was the same home he and her mother built.

It was the same nest her dad decided to crash.
It was the unrest he sat by in his new,

blue 1962 Ford he has just sold
himself. His red-skinned bald head falls,

bobs up, down on the round wheel. His crown
hits once, at least twenty times on the loud horn.

She's young and alone. It's dark. Her mother is gone.
The mother had turned forty and in her despair

left when she couldn't take this. Some weeks one
cannot bear to be there. But the daughter,

not knowing if he were alive or dead,
realized she had to get him out. With no words,

the couple came, and three helped him stagger in.
She was twenty, home from college in the summer.

He was forty-six, and died the next March. That hot
night, every one of the three persons who helped

merely went back to bed and never said one word.

Distance

scares Jan. Especially in men. It might
be like God's—it's always like Jan's dad's:

the time he drove her to school without speaking.
It is my fault, Jan thought. Though she knew he had

a hangover, he and her mother had fought.
But Jan thought: I've done wrong. Wrong. Wrong.

So wrong Jan willed to be strong. She willed to be
even stronger willed. To build her defenses.

Yet distance brings barricades, moats.
Guns poked through the castle walls. Finally, Jan

knows: distance brings armies face to face for nothing
except their final war.

To a Lighthouse

When the pistol went off while her son
was playing with his friend,
she knew it was her gun.
She did not know who had fired. Perhaps it was
the other boy, who had been quarreling
all along. Perhaps an outside intruder
on the set. Someone off the immediate
stage. Certainly not her husband, the father
who stood silent, Buddhist, on the edge.
In any case, her son's cheek did not bleed.
True, he had now lost a piece of flesh—

he has a hole he can never hide.

When she learns it was she who had shot him
in the dream, she is terribly distraught.
Could it be healed by surgery? No, No,
he says, Mom. He will live with it.
He is seven. His year for knowing comes.
Good. Evil. Good. Almost nothing is just one way.
He wants (like the boy in Virginia Woolf's novel)
to sail to a new place: a light house.
The novelist's character asks,
"Will the weather hold fine? Today or
tomorrow, how is the wind?"

TRUE LUMINOSITY

We watch one woman, two men, two little
thin girls at the edge of land and water
with its aquamarine, blue-green to azure
waves in May. White beach sand. North

Florida. They fly two rainbow kites
in late spring wind. It's 6:15 in the evening.
We two friends sit sipping wine, waiting for pink
sunset. "Today's a clear day," one of us says.

"This sun's not too hot." Little girls giggle,
run from one man's tight string back to theirs.
One Japanese-y, round, cylinder-like kite
tilts, flies high, as if it's true luminosity.

A kite shaped like a big blue bird flies too.
Real gray pelicans buzz in over the beach
in formations of sixes, beaks straight east.
But the colorful kites fly too high

in violet sky. Suddenly one man lets one kite
fly free, accidentally. The kite floats
right up into the sky—over white condo tops!
String catches in green palm trees too tall

to climb. He plots a plan to land it.
He fails. Finally, string loose, the kite flies
clear up to what was once imagined as God.
Iridescent kites flying up, out of sight.

The Decapolis

Here on the Sea of Galilee, I see
water where Peter walked, imagine storms.
That night, sleep in Kibbutz Magan with tens
of Hitler survivors. "Mr. Monday," who runs
the P. O., doesn't think I could know
about the Holocaust. Then he befriends me.
Takes me to see the fat lady in the dining room
who believes she is still starving. The stoic
man washing pots, who speaks only to his dog
since the camps. (His parents were taken when

he was three. He sat peeing in Paris.) Some
of our tour goes out on Gennesaret to eat
"St. Peter's fish." I am not hungry. Besides
the Jews, the voices of Jesus, his friends
call me. "Come back to heal me. Here,"
I say. But no reply. What else interests?
Water I swim in, how to wash clothes,
October flowers everywhere, sea-salt air,
the Golan Heights over toward the south
side of these hills. (We aren't far from Syria.)

New Jews settle. I've been here before
but never noticed ruins where ten
Hellenic cities sat: remains of all still rise
like the phoenix, flying up out of time. Twelve
fishermen who cast out for fish, for our
wounded souls, saw brashly-painted
Greek temples, hovering like neon haunts, holding
dozens of deities. How the called disciples
fought pagans. But the cities' death-fall came
tolling from earthquakes, through erosions,

sand-layers, eons of desert wind. Still,
they will not be defeated. Amid Arabs,
Israelis, against Jesus' legacy, tall,
phallic, the pillars still rise.
Out of context, seldom
pointed out to Christian pilgrims, ten temples'
pillars float like ghosts. Forever? Even
Demeter and Hades loom—as hot winter
winds blow toward this blue Israeli
October.

FLORIDA: GRAYTON BEACH
(for Carla)

To come to the same place more
than once with the same friend

is beyond mere blessing. To watch
water, aquamarine, perfectly clear,

year after year after year—even here
on Florida's panhandle white shore

is a gift. To swim in kaleidoscopic waves,
sip wine at sunset, snap shots

all cause me to recall my childhood
trips here in the fifties. To return is a wheel

of wonder I'd risk my life for. Beauty
but also repetition is the world's circle

revolving, I think, around sand, water,
dazzling earth-space. This pre-hurricane grace.

Labyrinth, Fourteen Ways

When you walk it,

    you are seldom lonely.

When you walk it,

    there are other people

on their own path. When

    you walk it with another,

you pay attention

    to your path—not to theirs.

When you walk with care,

    the two of you never collide.

When you walk it,

    you must look and listen.

When you walk it,

    you are by yourself—but not.

When you walk it,

    you get to a still-point.

When you get there,

    you are not finished yet.

When you arrive,

    and rest at the rose center,

you must exit as

    Christ did: down the Mount

of Transfiguration.

        To Jerusalem.

When you walk it,

    you have to trek and work your way out.

Recent Books from Pecan Grove Press

Barker, Wendy. *Between Frames*. 2006.
    ISBN: 1-931247-35-8 $9
Challender, Craig. *Dancing on Water*. 2005.
    ISBN: 1-931247-20-x $12
Davis, Glover. *Separate Lives*. 2007.
    ISBN: 1-931247-36-6 $12
Emmons, Jeanne. *Baseball Nights and DDT*. 2005.
    ISBN: 1-931247-26-9 $12.50
Essbaum, Jill Alexander. *Oh Forbidden*. 2005.
    ISBN: 1-931247-29-3 $9
Fargnoli, Patricia. *Small Songs of Pain*. 2004.
    ISBN: 1-931247-17-x $10
Gutierrez, Cesar. *Lonesome Pine*. 2006.
    ISBN: 1-931247-31-5 $9
Haddad, Marian. *Somewhere Between Mexico and a River Called Home*. 2004. ISBN: 1-931247-18-8 $15
Hochman, Will. *Freer*. 2006.
    ISBN: 1-931247-34-x $15
Hughes, Glenn. *Sleeping at the Open Window*. 2005.
    ISBN: 1-931247-25-0 $8
Hunley, Tom C. *My Life as a Minor Character*. 2005.
    ISBN: 1-931247-27-7 $8
Kasper, Catherine. *A Gradual Disappearance of Insects*. 2005.
    ISBN: 1-931247-22-6 $8
Kirkpatrick, Kathryn. *Beyond Reason*. 2004.
    ISBN: 1-931247-09-9 $12
McCann, Janet. *Emily's Dress*. 2004.
    ISBN: 1-931247-21-8 $8
McVay, Gwyn. Ordinary Beans. 2007.
    ISBN: 978-1-931247-39-9 $15
Mankiewicz, Angela Consolo. *An Eye*. 2006.
    ISBN: 1-931247-33-1 $9
Van Prooyen, Laura. *Inkblot and Altar*. 2006.
    ISBN: 1-931247-37-4 $9
Wayne, Jane O. *From the Nightstand*. 2007.
    ISBN: 1-931247-38-2 $15
Whitbread, Thomas. *The Structures Minds Erect*. 2007.
    ISBN: 978-1-931247-24-2 $15

For a complete listing of Pecan Grove Press titles,
please visit our website at *http://library.stmarytx.edu/pgpress*